Be Brave, Chester

A Baby Donkey's Story
Of
Courage and Friendship

Based on a True Story

By Karyl A. Price

i

ISBN: 978-0-9860830-0-6

Published by:
JIJ Born Again Publishing Co.
66486 E. 258 Road
Grove, OK 74344

Dedicated to:

My husband Richard~~
Who has helped
Me with the story,
Listened to my ideas,
And raised
Miniature Sicilian Donkey
As pets

And to my family~~
My two sons, Grady and Randy,
And my much-loved Grandchildren

Acknowledgements:

Many thanks to the following people:

M. Noonan for editing comments.
Richard Price for editing comments.
Parker for giving the first review of the book. (age 8)
Blaine, Savannah, and Anderson for reviewing the story and giving their comments. (ages 7-9)
Stephanie Jeffords for encouragement.
Randy Price for editing and formatting.
Grady Price for copyright.

In writing this book, I found Misty's words to be true.

Be Brave, Chester
A Story Of A Baby Donkey's Courage And Friendship

INTRODUCTION:

This story is based on a true event. The story is written as a children's book: as such, it is written from the viewpoint of the animals instead of the people.

All photos are taken from my photo albums; however, a few "word bubbles" are used in the book to complement a photo. One photo is a composite photo: the veterinary clinic waiting room which was constructed to illustrate information told us about Chester and his stay in the clinic. One photo is a cut-out photo of Tige the cat.

All of the other photos are as seen in my photo albums.

My husband, Richard Price absolutely loved the miniature Sicilian donkeys as pets. I gave three of the donkeys to him for Christmas in 1983. That was the start of the miniature Sicilian donkey herd and Chester's Story.

~~By Karyl (Carol is spelling used in book) Ann Price

Be Brave, Chester

Misty was a miniature Sicilian donkey. She loved her home on the Price Ranch with her herd and the other animals. She loved to see the green Tallgrass wave. She loved sniffing the wild flowers in the pasture. She loved exploring the dark woods.   She even loved checking out her people's backyard.

Richard and Carol Price were the people who fed her and petted her. She loved them, too.

Tige* was the Price's gray-striped cat. Tige always meowed at Misty to say "hello".
Misty would touch Tige with her nose. Tige would purr happily and rub against Misty's legs. Tige was her special cat friend.
*(Tige is pronounced like Tiger... just drop the 'ER' sound)

Tige

Just as winter was ending and spring beginning, Misty knew it was time for her to give birth to her baby donkey. Her belly was large and full. Misty left the herd to find a good suitable place on the property. She looked and looked. She found a

5

perfect spot in the pasture by the pond west
 of the white barn.

Misty whispered to the green grass peeking out of
the ground, "My baby will be born soon. Get ready
to greet him."

The green grass waved to her with joy. Early
spring yellow flowers bent toward her to hear
the good news, too. Misty was so happy waiting
for her foal* to be born. *(A baby donkey is called a foal.)

The next morning, Misty's baby donkey was born. Misty nuzzled him happily. "Your name is Chester," Misty brayed* his name for the first time.

(*Cats meow. Dogs bark. Donkeys bray. That is the name for their speech.)

She knew the flowers and the grass and wind and the sky had heard his name. She was so proud of Chester. She wanted to say his name over and over. "Chester. My baby Chester."

Chester looked up at his Mother with his big brown eyes. He looked around at the quiet prairie. He listened to the bird's singing. He saw the blue sky and the rising sun peeking out from behind a cloud. Sun rays bathed his body.

"This is a good place. I am glad I am here," Chester said.

Misty nuzzled him. "Stand up, Chester!" Misty said, "You must stand up now. You need to stand to get good milk for food."

Chester moved his legs. The newborn donkey twisted, and then he turned. "I can not stand up," He told his Mother. "I am trying. My front legs do not move!"

Misty felt alarmed.

She knew all baby donkeys stand on all four legs
immediately after being born. If Chester could not
stand, he would not get the milk he needed.
Something was wrong.
Something was very, very wrong.

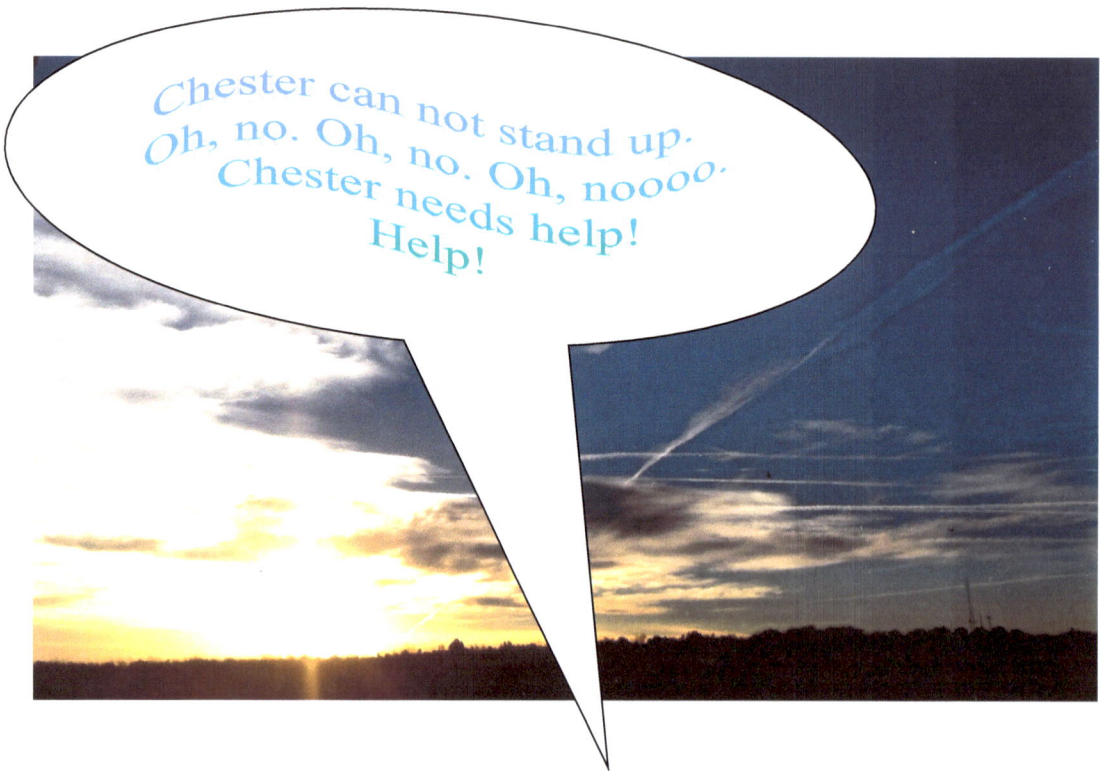

Chester can not stand up.
Oh, no. Oh, no. Oh, noooo.
Chester needs help!
Help!

Misty heard the wind whisper to the prairie
and woods around her, "Oh, no. Oh, no. Oh, no."

The sound echoed up to the clouds high in the sky.
"Chester can not stand up. Oh, no, Oh, no. Oh, no."

Misty drew back her head and gave a loud bray that shook the trees. Misty brayed, "Help. Help. People...come help me. Come help me quickly. My baby must have your help!"

Richard and Carol heard Misty give an alarm bray. Misty's people came running to see what was wrong. Richard saw the foal on the ground beside Misty. Chester's front legs were crooked and bent. Richard gently stroked the baby donkey's damp furry coat of hair.

"Misty's foal has something wrong," Richard told Carol. "Go get the farm truck. Chester needs the veterinary* in town right now.
Hurry. You must hurry."
(* A veterinary is a big word for an animal doctor.)

Misty did not understand what the people were saying, but she saw Richard lifting Chester up from the ground. Misty told her baby donkey, "My people always take good care of me. They will help you."

Misty brayed loudly to Chester,
"Be brave. Just be brave."

Chester felt himself shaking with fright. Chester looked at Misty helplessly. Chester looked at the green waving grass in the distance. "The grass is waving to tell me to be brave."

Then he looked at the yellow flowers... on the near-by hillside. "The flowers are curving their stems. Yes, the flowers are writing the words...be brave."

Chester heard the wind. "Yes. Yes. The wind is whispering...be brave."

Chester told his Mother, "I will try to be brave."

Carol quickly arrived with the farm truck. Richard put the frightened foal into Carol's arms. Misty followed the truck as far as the gate, braying to Chester with each step. She stayed by the fence and watched as the truck drove down the road with her baby inside it.

Misty dug her hooves into the ground for a long, long wait. She wanted to wait until Chester came home again. But Misty knew she had to trust her people. Misty had to be brave herself.

Misty brayed to the patchy grass by the road and the flowers and the wind, "My people know what to do. I have seen them bottle feed other baby animals. They will feed my baby and fix his legs. My baby will be OK."

Chester looked back at his Mother from the farm truck window. Oh, he wanted to be with her.

His Mother looked smaller and smaller until he could no longer see her.

Misty looked for her son. Finally, all she could see were Chester's ears and a part of his forehead. The truck was moving farther and farther away from her. Misty could see Carol cuddling Chester.

"Chester will be OK," Misty told herself again.

Carol petted Chester's forehead. She cuddled him up against her body. "Don't be scared," She said in a soothing voice.

 Carol took one last look at Misty standing bravely by the fence as Richard opened the gate. Carol knew it would be difficult for Misty also.

Chester could not see his Mother anymore.
But he remembered the grass waving "Be brave" to him and remembered his Mother's words. "My people will help you walk, Chester."
He whispered, "I will try to be brave."

Chester felt the truck stop. Richard carried the foal into the waiting room of Liz, the animal doctor.

Animals were everywhere. Chester did not know what cats were or what dogs were or what birds were. Meows, barks, shrieks: sounds filled the room from floor to ceiling with noise. Too much noise! Chester wanted to cover his ears, but he couldn't.

Chester saw three large animals making a menacing sound. Their sounds were very loud, and the people called them dogs. Chester did not want the dogs to even see him. Then he told himself, "The dogs are just so big and scary. What can I do so they do not see me?"

What if I roll into a ball? Chester thought to himself... He was glad that Richard was there.

"Dr. Liz," Richard said to a woman in a white coat. "This is our newborn donkey. Look at his knees. Something is wrong."

Chester remembered the flowers twisting their stems and writing "Be brave" to him. He remembered his Mother's words, "Be brave." Chester told himself, "That person Dr. Liz will help me walk. I will be brave."

Richard carried Chester into a quiet room and placed the scared donkey on a white table there.

Chester moved around frantically in Richard's arms. Chester felt Richard holding him so he would not fall off.

Dr. Liz came into the room. She talked to Chester and petted him. Then she handled his knee joints. Dr. Liz told Richard, "His knee joints are not right. The donkey will need an operation. His knees can be fixed, but he will have to stay here for some time."

Chester did not understand what operation meant. But Chester heard the kindness in Dr. Liz's voice. Chester told himself, "Yes, I am in the right place. Even the wind whispered to me to be brave. I will try."

Then Chester saw a person in a white coat with a thin something in her hand. She touched Chester with the needle. Chester's eyes began to close. When Chester woke up, he looked at his legs. His legs did not look like his legs at all! "Oh, what have they done to me? My legs are not my legs!"

Each front leg was bandaged with a plastic splint on them.

Soon, Dr. Liz came into the room. She petted the donkey and told her assistant, "Drip milk in the donkey's mouth, and then call Richard Price. Chester's doing fine."

Chester was taken to a larger area. He was lowered down to the floor.   His knees were not like his knees. Richard and Carol and the doctor were gone, and he was alone with the doctor's assistant, "Where am I now? What will happen here?"

Chester keep repeating his Mother's words, "Mother told me to be brave. I <u>must</u> <u>be</u> <u>brave</u>." The words fought away the fear. Dr. Liz's assistant put something on his tongue. It was good, and it made his stomach feel better. Chester was hungry but didn't know it.

Carefully, the assistant dripped milk in his mouth until Chester grabbed the bottle's tip with his mouth and sucked up the warm, refreshing fluid. Chester felt better all over.

"Oh!" Chester thought, "That was good. I want that often. I was brave, and the people helped me."

Chester did not want the assistant to leave, but the assistant did. Chester was left totally alone in the room. He was scared again. But every time he was scared now, he repeated his Mother's words, "Be brave. Be brave." With a full stomach, and not much pain in his legs, Chester curled up with his head resting on his body and fell asleep.

That night, Chester dreamed he could stand up and walk without the big bandages and the plastic splints on his legs.

Chester dreamed ...

Chester dreamed he was both brave and well.

When he woke up, the fear left slowly, but Chester knew he would be OK. The people were helping him. He tried pulling his front legs under him. He twisted and turned, but he still could not stand up.

The assistant came several times each day and fed him from a bottle. She petted him and talked to him. Chester was growing stronger from the nourishing milk and good care.

  Then only a few short days later, Chester stood up.

He placed one leg in front of the other, and Chester walked!

Chester brayed, "I want to go home now.
I want to show my Mother how brave I am."

Chester did not know the bandages and splints would be on his legs for a long, long time. He thought the doctor would take them off now that he could walk. Chester wanted to walk with his Mother to the place where he had been born.

Chester could imagine them walking together! It was a wonderful thought.

Dr. Liz's assistant came and removed the splint and bandages. She then put salve on his surgery cuts and put the splints back on. The salve always stung his skin. He tried to be brave, but Chester could not.

But then....Chester was taken to the front of the building where Dr. Liz's office was. Richard was waiting for him.

Chester remembered Richard.

The doctor explained to Richard that people at the clinic held Chester on their lap or petted him. So Richard put Chester on his lap and held him, too.

"I must be going home." Chester thought, "All the animals are saying good-bye to me. I will see my Mother soon. I am going home."

He brayed as loudly as he could.

Richard and Carol were ready to take Chester home.

Dr. Liz gave Richard and Carol instructions for his care, "You must change his bandages twice a day. Take off the splint and rewrap the knee. Place this medicine on the surgery cut and keep it clean."

Chester did not know what the doctor said. But he saw her hand Richard the salve; Chester knew he did not like it. The salve also meant his splints were not coming off!

But Chester felt brave and happy anyway.

Richard picked Chester up, took him to the farm truck, and placed him on Carol's lap.

Chester remembered the truck and
Carol holding him before,
"I am going home!
I'll see my Mother."

Chester brayed with joy even if
he was going home with his legs
still in splints.

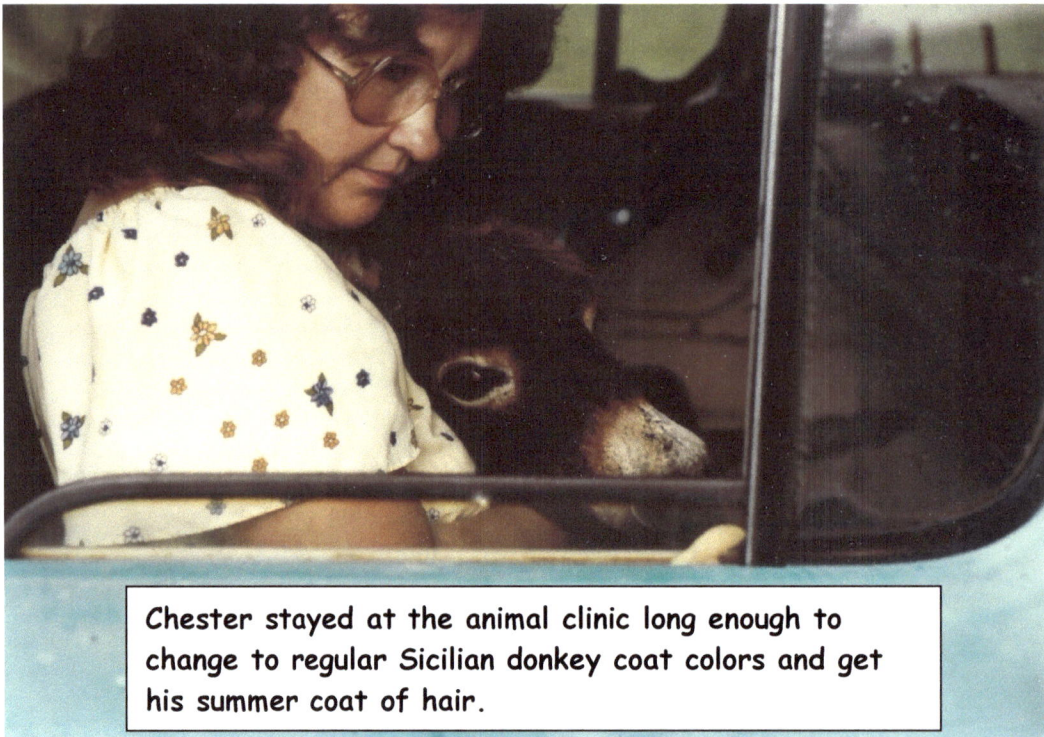

Chester stayed at the animal clinic long enough to change to regular Sicilian donkey coat colors and get his summer coat of hair.

Chester remembered the gravel road to the ranch house.

He remembered the green grass and the flowers. The grass and flowers filled all the pasture now and were waving "hello" to him.

Then Chester saw his Mother. Most of all, Chester remembered his beloved Mother.

Misty left the herd and ran to the truck. She brayed happily to him, "Welcome home, son. I love you, son. I missed you so much." Richard lifted Chester off Carol's lap and put him down on all of his four legs.

Misty and Chester rubbed their necks together with happiness. Misty was so happy to see that her foal was OK. Chester moved back and forth for his Mother to show her that he could walk.

Chester brayed proudly, "I was brave, and now I can stand up. I can walk. Yes, I can. See my splints. They help me walk! Yes, they do." Chester was brave about his splints. Seeing his Mother helped him be brave.

Chester grew stronger each day by following the herd. He was last behind his Mother and the herd wherever they went, but he could walk.

Chester always managed to go where they went. Chester walked across the pasture. Chester walked through the woods. Chester walked to the pond to get a drink of water. Chester was so proud that he could walk, even if it was a struggle to move his legs forward quickly.

But Chester was still unhappy when his bandages were changed. Chester struggled every time Richard changed them. He twisted and turned. He tried to be brave, but Chester always remembered the salve.

Misty's friend, Tige the cat, and Misty watched from behind the fence when Richard changed Chester's bandages. They felt sorry for Chester, and both wanted to help.

Tige remembered how his Mother comforted him by purring with him. Misty could not go over, through, or under the fence, but Tige knew he could crawl under the fence to Chester! Tige knew how to help.

The next day, Chester was twisting around again to avoid the salve. Tige crept up to Chester, laid down on Chester neck, and purred the loudest purr he could purr.

Chester liked the warmth of Tige's fur against his neck. He liked Tige's steady purr, purr, purr, purr.

"Oh, my!" Chester said. "Even Tige is helping. My Mother is braying at me to be brave. Tige is purring to me. I will be brave."

He liked Tige's purr so much that he did not remember the salve at all. Richard could easily change the bandage now. Chester did not move, and he did not struggle at all. Chester was happy that Tige the cat helped him.

Each day, Tige curled up on Chester's neck and purred during every bandage change. He came every day for all that summer and fall until Chester was well, and the splints were taken off Chester's front knee joints. That took a long time, but Chester was finally well.

Chester could now play and run like the other animals.

The grass waving, the flowers writing, the wind whispering, his Mother's words of encouragement and now Tige the cat purring--Chester knew they all helped him to get well and be brave.   He had conquered all of his fear with their help. Chester knew he was brave now.

Misty, Chester, and Tige all remained best friends for the rest of their lives on the ranch.

With his very best bray, Chester says to each one of you who has read or listened to his story:

"Good-bye. My wish is for a happy life for all of you children. And always remember: be brave, no matter what happens."

If you are reading this story for a class reading assignment, you might want some discussion topics. Here is a list for you.

Discussion Topics:

1. Why do you think Chester and Tige became friends?
2. How did Misty know Chester needed her people to help him?
3. Why is it important to help others as Tige helped Chester?
4. How were Tige, Chester, or Misty brave?
5. What does "being brave" mean?
6. What was scary about Doctor Liz's waiting room?
7. How were Tige and Chester alike?
8. Which character in the story do you like the most?
9. Which character in the story seems to be the most like you?
10. If Chester could be here with us, what would you say to him?
11. What do we learn from Chester in this story?
12. What does this story say to you?

CHESTER'S PHOTO ALBUM

By fall, Chester was back with the herd. He was ready for winter. The donkeys often stayed with the cattle herd.

CHESTER'S PHOTO ALBUM

Misty and Chester walking with the herd
after bandages removed.

CHESTER'S PHOTO ALBUM

Just like children, donkeys like to try to read.
 I think they see the people with a newspaper or book,
and they want to see why that captures our attention.
The photo is of Richard and Chester's father.

CHESTER'S PHOTO ALBUM

Winter meant snow, and Chester was tracking through the snow as his legs were healing. But Chester was now so brave that he walked through the snow with very few problems. He kept up with the herd.

CHESTER'S PHOTO ALBUM

All of Misty's foals always had the sometimes brown, sometimes black distinctive cross marking on the Sicilian donkey's back, running all the length from tail tip to head--then across a foot or so down both the sides of the front legs.

CHESTER'S PHOTO ALBUM

Donkeys are herd animals. Chester quickly readapted to the herd. As his legs healed, he was able to keep up with their walking pace most of the time. His splints were off by fall.

Our Herd of Miniature Sicilian Donkeys

We were not there during the time Chester was in the clinic. However, we have tried to recreate some of the happenings inside the clinic from what Dr. Liz, our veterinarian, told us:

Chester was difficult to keep inside the stalls for other farm animals. Although he could not stand up, he learned to scoot his body under the fence, and so as soon as he could stand, Dr. Liz removed him to the front of the building and placed him in her large office. He loved to sit on someone's lap after he came home, so apparently, someone held him on their lap a lot at the clinic.

Chester learned to really like cats at the clinic; however, in general, our donkeys liked cats. They liked dogs less but accepted them also. They also liked to be in a herd with cattle some of the time. They were definitely a herd animal. As such, they were calm, placid, and very intelligent.

Our Miniature Sicilian Donkeys were tame, usually from birth. They were social animals and especially become very attached to people. Ours followed us around, wanted to be petted constantly, and liked to lay their head on our lap or arm if they were standing next to us.

When we would be at work, some of our donkeys would always slip under our fence just to be with the neighbors' children. They would come back in the evening.   The children told us the donkeys just wanted to be petted, hugged, eat something from their hand, then they would go back to our farm after that.

Our Sicilian Donkeys were very careful not to hurt people; they used their lips to pick up food from our open hand rather than using their teeth. However, we always fed them food from the palm of our hand and did not hold food up with our fingers.

They wanted to be with people as much as they could. They would sometimes tug at our shirt or coat if we were ignoring them and not petting them enough.

We would advise, though, that a child should be watched over by an adult when the child tries to pet or feed a Miniature Sicilian Donkey. Use the normal precautions you would use with any other animal or pet.

Our experiences with the Miniature Sicilian Donkeys are based upon our raising them for over 20 years and verified by the stories we were told from people who bought the donkeys from us.

Just think of them as super-smart pets who want affection most of the time.

~~Richard and Karyl (Carol) Price

www.ingramcontent.com/pod-product-compliance
Lightning Source LLC
Chambersburg PA
CBHW061354090426
42739CB00002B/26